GET SHIT DONE!

Monthly/Weekly Planner with Inspirational Quotes
(5"x8")

2010

This Planner Belongs To:

_____

Phone:

D1509600

E-mail:

IMPORTANT CONTACTS

👤	👤
☏	☏
✉	✉
📪	📪

👤	👤
☏	☏
✉	✉
📪	📪

👤	👤
☏	☏
✉	✉
📪	📪

IMPORTANT DATES

2019

JANUARY
s	m	t	w	t	f	s
		1	2	3	4	5
6	7	8	9	10	11	12
13	14	15	16	17	18	19
20	21	22	23	24	25	26
27	28	29	30	31		

FEBRUARY
s	m	t	w	t	f	s
					1	2
3	4	5	6	7	8	9
10	11	12	13	14	15	16
17	18	19	20	21	22	23
24	25	26	27	28		

MARCH
s	m	t	w	t	f	s
					1	2
3	4	5	6	7	8	9
10	11	12	13	14	15	16
17	18	19	20	21	22	23
24	25	26	27	28	29	30
31						

APRIL
s	m	t	w	t	f	s
	1	2	3	4	5	6
7	8	9	10	11	12	13
14	15	16	17	18	19	20
21	22	23	24	25	26	27
28	29	30				

MAY
s	m	t	w	t	f	s
			1	2	3	4
5	6	7	8	9	10	11
12	13	14	15	16	17	18
19	20	21	22	23	24	25
26	27	28	29	30	31	

JUNE
s	m	t	w	t	f	s
						1
2	3	4	5	6	7	8
9	10	11	12	13	14	15
16	17	18	19	20	21	22
23	24	25	26	27	28	29
30						

JULY
s	m	t	w	t	f	s
	1	2	3	4	5	6
7	8	9	10	11	12	13
14	15	16	17	18	19	20
21	22	23	24	25	26	27
28	29	30	31			

AUGUST
s	m	t	w	t	f	s
				1	2	3
4	5	6	7	8	9	10
11	12	13	14	15	16	17
18	19	20	21	22	23	24
25	26	27	28	29	30	31

SEPTEMBER
s	m	t	w	t	f	s
1	2	3	4	5	6	7
8	9	10	11	12	13	14
15	16	17	18	19	20	21
22	23	24	25	26	27	28
29	30					

OCTOBER
s	m	t	w	t	f	s
		1	2	3	4	5
6	7	8	9	10	11	12
13	14	15	16	17	18	19
20	21	22	23	24	25	26
27	28	29	30	31		

NOVEMBER
s	m	t	w	t	f	s
					1	2
3	4	5	6	7	8	9
10	11	12	13	14	15	16
17	18	19	20	21	22	23
24	25	26	27	28	29	30

DECEMBER
s	m	t	w	t	f	s
1	2	3	4	5	6	7
8	9	10	11	12	13	14
15	16	17	18	19	20	21
22	23	24	25	26	27	28
29	30	31				

HOLIDAYS

- New Year's Day (January 1)
- Birthday of Martin Luther King, Jr. (January 21)
- Washington's Birthday (February 18)
- Memorial Day (May 27)
- Independence Day (July 4)
- Labor Day (September 2)
- Columbus Day (October 14)
- Veterans Day (November 11)
- Thanksgiving Day (November 28)
- Christmas Day (December 25)

January

Sunday	Monday	Tuesday	Wednesday
30	31	01 *New Year's Day*	02
06	07	08	09
13	14	15	16
20	21 *Birthday of Martin Luther King, Jr.*	22	23
27	28	29	30
03	04	05	06

Thursday	Friday	Saturday	To Do:
03	04	05	☐
			☐
			☐
10	11	12	☐
			☐
			☐
			☐
17	18	19	☐
			☐
			☐
			☐
24	25	26	☐
			☐
			☐
			☐
31	01	02	☐
			☐
			☐
			☐
07	08	09	☐
			☐
			☐
			☐

December
The Week Of December 31, 2018

Monday *(31)*

- [ ]
- [ ]
- [ ]

Tuesday *(1)*

- [ ]
- [ ]
- [ ]

Wednesday *(2)*

- [ ]
- [ ]
- [ ]

Thursday *(3)*

- [ ]
- [ ]
- [ ]

Friday *(4)*

- [ ]
- [ ]
- [ ]

Saturday/Sunday *(5 & 6)*

- [ ]
- [ ]
- [ ]

Life shrinks or expands in proportion to one's courage.
-Anais Nin

Top Priority for the Week:

To Do:

☐   ☐

☐   ☐

☐   ☐

☐   ☐

Appointments:

☐   ☐

☐   ☐

☐   ☐

Carryover from Prior Week:

☐

☐

☐

Habit Tracker	S	M	T	W	H	F	S

Notes

JANUARY

s	m	t	w	t	f	s
		1	2	3	4	5
6	7	8	9	10	11	12
13	14	15	16	17	18	19
20	21	22	23	24	25	26
27	28	29	30	31		

January
The Week Of January 7, 2018

Monday *(7)*

- [ ]
- [ ]
- [ ]

Tuesday *(8)*

- [ ]
- [ ]
- [ ]

Wednesday *(9)*

- [ ]
- [ ]
- [ ]

Thursday *(10)*

- [ ]
- [ ]
- [ ]

Friday *(11)*

- [ ]
- [ ]
- [ ]

Saturday/Sunday *(12 & 13)*

- [ ]
- [ ]
- [ ]

If you can dream it, you can achieve it. -Zig Ziglar

Top Priority for the Week:

To Do:
- [ ]   [ ]
- [ ]   [ ]
- [ ]   [ ]
- [ ]   [ ]

Appointments:
- [ ]   [ ]
- [ ]   [ ]
- [ ]   [ ]

Carryover from Prior Week:
- [ ]
- [ ]
- [ ]

Habit Tracker	S	M	T	W	H	F	S

Notes

JANUARY

s	m	t	w	t	f	s
		1	2	3	4	5
6	7	8	9	10	11	12
13	14	15	16	17	18	19
20	21	22	23	24	25	26
27	28	29	30	31		

January
The Week Of January 14, 2019

Monday *(14)*

☐

☐

☐

Tuesday *(15)*

☐

☐

☐

Wednesday *(16)*

☐

☐

☐

Thursday *(17)*

☐

☐

☐

Friday *(18)*

☐

☐

☐

Saturday/Sunday *(19 & 20)*

☐

☐

☐

Storms makes tress take deeper roots.

Top Priority for the Week:

To Do:
- [ ]   - [ ]
- [ ]   - [ ]
- [ ]   - [ ]
- [ ]   - [ ]

Appointments:
- [ ]   - [ ]
- [ ]   - [ ]
- [ ]   - [ ]

Carryover from Prior Week:
- [ ]
- [ ]
- [ ]

Habit Tracker	S	M	T	W	H	F	S

Notes

▌ JANUARY

s	m	t	w	t	f	s
		1	2	3	4	5
6	7	8	9	10	11	12
13	14	15	16	17	18	19
20	21	22	23	24	25	26
27	28	29	30	31		

January
The Week Of January 21, 2019

Monday *(21)*

☐

☐

☐

Tuesday *(22)*

☐

☐

☐

Wednesday *(23)*

☐

☐

☐

Thursday *(24)*

☐

☐

☐

Friday *(25)*

☐

☐

☐

Saturday/Sunday *(26 & 27)*

☐

☐

☐

Top Priority for the Week:

To Do:

☐   ☐

☐   ☐

☐   ☐

☐   ☐

Appointments:

☐   ☐

☐   ☐

☐   ☐

Carryover from Prior Week:

☐

☐

☐

Habit Tracker	S	M	T	W	H	F	S

Notes

▌JANUARY

s	m	t	w	t	f	s
		1	2	3	4	5
6	7	8	9	10	11	12
13	14	15	16	17	18	19
20	21	22	23	24	25	26
27	28	29	30	31		

January
The Week Of January 28, 2019

Monday *(28)*

☐

☐

☐

Tuesday *(29)*

☐

☐

☐

Wednesday *(30)*

☐

☐

☐

Thursday *(31)*

☐

☐

☐

Friday *(1)*

☐

☐

☐

Saturday/Sunday *(2 & 3)*

☐

☐

☐

Eighty percent of success is showing up.

Top Priority for the Week:

To Do:
☐
☐
☐
☐
☐
☐
☐
☐

Appointments:
☐
☐
☐
☐
☐
☐

Carryover from Prior Week:
☐
☐
☐

Habit Tracker	S	M	T	W	H	F	S

Notes

FEBRUARY

s	m	t	w	t	f	s
					1	2
3	4	5	6	7	8	9
10	11	12	13	14	15	16
17	18	19	20	21	22	23
24	25	26	27	28		

February

Sunday	Monday	Tuesday	Wednesday
27	28	29	30
03	04	05	06
10	11	12	13
17	18 *Washington's Birthday*	19	20
24	25	26	27
03	04	05	06

Thursday	Friday	Saturday	To Do:
31	01	02	☐
			☐
			☐
07	08	09	☐
			☐
			☐
			☐
14	15	16	☐
Valentines Day			☐
			☐
21	22	23	☐
			☐
			☐
			☐
28	01	02	☐
			☐
			☐
			☐
07	08	09	☐
			☐
			☐
			☐

February
The Week Of February 4, 2019

Monday *(4)*

- [ ]
- [ ]
- [ ]

Tuesday *(5)*

- [ ]
- [ ]
- [ ]

Wednesday *(6)*

- [ ]
- [ ]
- [ ]

Thursday *(7)*

- [ ]
- [ ]
- [ ]

Friday *(8)*

- [ ]
- [ ]
- [ ]

Saturday/Sunday *(9 & 10)*

- [ ]
- [ ]
- [ ]

An obstacle is often a stepping stone. -Prescott Bush

Top Priority for the Week:

To Do:

☐   ☐

☐   ☐

☐   ☐

☐   ☐

Appointments:

☐   ☐

☐   ☐

☐   ☐

Carryover from Prior Week:

☐

☐

☐

Habit Tracker	S	M	T	W	H	F	S

Notes

_____

_____

_____

_____

_____

FEBRUARY

s	m	t	w	t	f	s
					1	2
3	4	5	6	7	8	9
10	11	12	13	14	15	16
17	18	19	20	21	22	23
24	25	26	27	28		

February
The Week Of February 11, 2019

Monday *(11)*

☐

☐

☐

Tuesday *(12)*

☐

☐

☐

Wednesday *(13)*

☐

☐

☐

Thursday *(14)*

☐

☐

☐

Friday *(15)*

☐

☐

☐

Saturday/Sunday *(16 & 17)*

☐

☐

☐

Faith can move mountains.

Top Priority for the Week:

To Do:
- [ ]   [ ]
- [ ]   [ ]
- [ ]   [ ]
- [ ]   [ ]

Appointments:
- [ ]   [ ]
- [ ]   [ ]
- [ ]   [ ]

Carryover from Prior Week:
- [ ]
- [ ]
- [ ]

Habit Tracker	S	M	T	W	H	F	S

Notes

■ **FEBRUARY**

s	m	t	w	t	f	s
					1	2
3	4	5	6	7	8	9
10	11	12	13	14	15	16
17	18	19	20	21	22	23
24	25	26	27	28		

February
The Week Of February 18, 2019

Monday *(18)*

- [ ]
- [ ]
- [ ]

Tuesday *(19)*

- [ ]
- [ ]
- [ ]

Wednesday *(20)*

- [ ]
- [ ]
- [ ]

Thursday *(21)*

- [ ]
- [ ]
- [ ]

Friday *(22)*

- [ ]
- [ ]
- [ ]

Saturday/Sunday *(23 & 24)*

- [ ]
- [ ]
- [ ]

The distance between your dreams and reality is call action.

Top Priority for the Week:

To Do:
☐   ☐

☐   ☐

☐   ☐

☐   ☐

Appointments:

☐   ☐

☐   ☐

☐   ☐

Carryover from Prior Week:

☐

☐

☐

Habit Tracker	S	M	T	W	H	F	S

Notes

■ FEBRUARY

s	m	t	w	t	f	s
					1	2
3	4	5	6	7	8	9
10	11	12	13	14	15	16
17	18	19	20	21	22	23
24	25	26	27	28		

February
The Week Of February 25, 2019

Monday *(25)*

☐

☐

☐

Tuesday *(26)*

☐

☐

☐

Wednesday *(27)*

☐

☐

☐

Thursday *(28)*

☐

☐

☐

Friday *(1)*

☐

☐

☐

Saturday/Sunday *(2 & 3)*

☐

☐

☐

Climb mountains to see lowlands. -Chinese Proverb

Top Priority for the Week:

To Do:
- [ ]
- [ ]
- [ ]
- [ ]
- [ ]
- [ ]
- [ ]
- [ ]

Appointments:
- [ ]
- [ ]
- [ ]
- [ ]
- [ ]
- [ ]

Carryover from Prior Week:
- [ ]
- [ ]
- [ ]

Habit Tracker	S	M	T	W	H	F	S

Notes
_____
_____
_____
_____
_____

MARCH

s	m	t	w	t	f	s
					1	2
3	4	5	6	7	8	9
10	11	12	13	14	15	16
17	18	19	20	21	22	23
24	25	26	27	28	29	30
31						

March

Sunday	Monday	Tuesday	Wednesday
24	25	26	27
03	04	05	06
10	11	12	13
17 *St. Patrick's Day*	18	19	20
24	25	26	27
31	01	02	03

Thursday	Friday	Saturday	To Do:
28	01	02	☐
			☐
			☐
07	08	09	☐
			☐
			☐
			☐
14	15	16	☐
			☐
			☐
			☐
21	22	23	☐
			☐
			☐
28	29	30	☐
			☐
			☐
			☐
04	05	06	☐
			☐
			☐
			☐

March
The Week Of March 4, 2019

Monday *(4)*

- [ ]
- [ ]
- [ ]

Tuesday *(5)*

- [ ]
- [ ]
- [ ]

Wednesday *(6)*

- [ ]
- [ ]
- [ ]

Thursday *(7)*

- [ ]
- [ ]
- [ ]

Friday *(8)*

- [ ]
- [ ]
- [ ]

Saturday/Sunday *(9 & 10)*

- [ ]
- [ ]
- [ ]

Courage doesn't always roar. -Mary Anne Radmacher

Top Priority for the Week:

To Do:
☐   ☐

☐   ☐

☐   ☐

☐   ☐

Appointments:

☐   ☐

☐   ☐

☐   ☐

Carryover from Prior Week:

☐

☐

☐

Habit Tracker	S	M	T	W	H	F	S

Notes
_____

_____

_____

_____

_____

▎MARCH

s	m	t	w	t	f	s
					1	2
3	4	5	6	7	8	9
10	11	12	13	14	15	16
17	18	19	20	21	22	23
24	25	26	27	28	29	30
31						

March
The Week Of March 11, 2019

Monday *(11)*

☐

☐

☐

Tuesday *(12)*

☐

☐

☐

Wednesday *(13)*

☐

☐

☐

Thursday *(14)*

☐

☐

☐

Friday *(15)*

☐

☐

☐

Saturday/Sunday *(16 & 17)*

☐

☐

☐

Fall seven times and stand up eight. -Japanese Proverb

Top Priority for the Week:

To Do:
- [ ]
- [ ]
- [ ]
- [ ]
- [ ]
- [ ]
- [ ]
- [ ]

Appointments:
- [ ]
- [ ]
- [ ]
- [ ]
- [ ]
- [ ]

Carryover from Prior Week:
- [ ]
- [ ]
- [ ]

Habit Tracker	S	M	T	W	H	F	S

Notes

▌MARCH

s	m	t	w	t	f	s
					1	2
3	4	5	6	7	8	9
10	11	12	13	14	15	16
17	18	19	20	21	22	23
24	25	26	27	28	29	30
31						

March
The Week Of March 18, 2019

Monday *(18)*

☐

☐

☐

Tuesday *(19)*

☐

☐

☐

Wednesday *(20)*

☐

☐

☐

Thursday *(21)*

☐

☐

☐

Friday *(22)*

☐

☐

☐

Saturday/Sunday *(23 & 24)*

☐

☐

☐

The secret of getting ahead is getting started. -Sally Berger

Top Priority for the Week:

To Do:
☐   ☐

☐   ☐

☐   ☐

☐   ☐

Appointments:

☐   ☐

☐   ☐

☐   ☐

Carryover from Prior Week:

☐

☐

☐

Habit Tracker	S	M	T	W	H	F	S

Notes

▌MARCH

s	m	t	w	t	f	s
					1	2
3	4	5	6	7	8	9
10	11	12	13	14	15	16
17	18	19	20	21	22	23
24	25	26	27	28	29	30
31						

March

The Week Of March 25, 2019

Monday *(25)*

☐

☐

☐

Tuesday *(26)*

☐

☐

☐

Wednesday *(27)*

☐

☐

☐

Thursday *(28)*

☐

☐

☐

Friday *(29)*

☐

☐

☐

Saturday/Sunday *(30 & 31)*

☐

☐

☐

Bravery means finding something more important than fear.

Top Priority for the Week:

To Do:
- ☐
- ☐
- ☐
- ☐

- ☐
- ☐
- ☐
- ☐

Appointments:
- ☐
- ☐
- ☐

- ☐
- ☐
- ☐

Carryover from Prior Week:
- ☐
- ☐
- ☐

Habit Tracker	S	M	T	W	H	F	S

Notes
_____

_____

_____

_____

_____

APRIL

s	m	t	w	t	f	s
	1	2	3	4	5	6
7	8	9	10	11	12	13
14	15	16	17	18	19	20
21	22	23	24	25	26	27
28	29	30				

April

Sunday	Monday	Tuesday	Wednesday
31	01	02	03
07	08	09	10
14	15	16	17
21	22	23	24
28	29	30	01
05	06	07	08

Thursday	Friday	Saturday	To Do:
04	05	06	☐
			☐
			☐
			☐
11	12	13	☐
			☐
			☐
			☐
18	19	20	☐
			☐
			☐
			☐
25	26	27	☐
			☐
			☐
			☐
02	03	04	☐
			☐
			☐
			☐
09	10	11	☐
			☐
			☐
			☐

April
The Week Of April 1, 2019

Monday *(1)*

- [ ]
- [ ]
- [ ]

Tuesday *(2)*

- [ ]
- [ ]
- [ ]

Wednesday *(3)*

- [ ]
- [ ]
- [ ]

Thursday *(4)*

- [ ]
- [ ]
- [ ]

Friday *(5)*

- [ ]
- [ ]
- [ ]

Saturday/Sunday *(6 & 7)*

- [ ]
- [ ]
- [ ]

> I never dream of success. I worked for it. -Estee Lauder

Top Priority for the Week:

To Do:

☐   ☐

☐   ☐

☐   ☐

☐   ☐

Appointments:

☐   ☐

☐   ☐

☐   ☐

Carryover from Prior Week:

☐

☐

☐

Habit Tracker	S	M	T	W	H	F	S

Notes

_____

_____

_____

_____

_____

APRIL

s	m	t	w	t	f	s
	1	2	3	4	5	6
7	8	9	10	11	12	13
14	15	16	17	18	19	20
21	22	23	24	25	26	27
28	29	30				

April

The Week Of April 8, 2019

Monday *(8)*

☐

☐

☐

Tuesday *(9)*

☐

☐

☐

Wednesday *(10)*

☐

☐

☐

Thursday *(11)*

☐

☐

☐

Friday *(12)*

☐

☐

☐

Saturday/Sunday *(13 & 14)*

☐

☐

☐

Adversity is the first path to truth. -Lord Byron

Top Priority for the Week:

To Do:
☐
☐
☐
☐
☐
☐
☐
☐

Appointments:
☐
☐
☐
☐
☐
☐

Carryover from Prior Week:
☐
☐
☐

Habit Tracker	S	M	T	W	H	F	S

Notes

APRIL

s	m	t	w	t	f	s
	1	2	3	4	5	6
7	8	9	10	11	12	13
14	15	16	17	18	19	20
21	22	23	24	25	26	27
28	29	30				

April
The Week Of April 15, 2019

Monday *(15)*

☐

☐

☐

Tuesday *(16)*

☐

☐

☐

Wednesday *(17)*

☐

☐

☐

Thursday *(18)*

☐

☐

☐

Friday *(19)*

☐

☐

☐

Saturday/Sunday *(20 & 21)*

☐

☐

☐

Every accomplishment starts with the decision to try.
-John F. Kennedy

Top Priority for the Week:

To Do:
☐   ☐

☐   ☐

☐   ☐

☐   ☐

Appointments:
☐   ☐

☐   ☐

☐   ☐

Carryover from Prior Week:
☐

☐

☐

Habit Tracker	S	M	T	W	H	F	S

Notes

_____

_____

_____

_____

_____

▌ APRIL

s	m	t	w	t	f	s
	1	2	3	4	5	6
7	8	9	10	11	12	13
14	15	16	17	18	19	20
21	22	23	24	25	26	27
28	29	30				

April

The Week Of April 22, 2019

Monday *(22)*

☐

☐

☐

Tuesday *(23)*

☐

☐

☐

Wednesday *(24)*

☐

☐

☐

Thursday *(25)*

☐

☐

☐

Friday *(26)*

☐

☐

☐

Saturday/Sunday *(27 & 28)*

☐

☐

☐

Top Priority for the Week:

To Do:
- [ ]
- [ ]
- [ ]
- [ ]

- [ ]
- [ ]
- [ ]
- [ ]

Appointments:

- [ ]
- [ ]
- [ ]

- [ ]
- [ ]
- [ ]

Carryover from Prior Week:

- [ ]
- [ ]
- [ ]

Habit Tracker	S	M	T	W	H	F	S

Notes

APRIL						
s	m	t	w	t	f	s
	1	2	3	4	5	6
7	8	9	10	11	12	13
14	15	16	17	18	19	20
21	22	23	24	25	26	27
28	29	30				

April
The Week Of April 29, 2019

Monday *(29)*

☐

☐

☐

Tuesday *(30)*

☐

☐

☐

Wednesday *(1)*

☐

☐

☐

Thursday *(2)*

☐

☐

☐

Friday *(3)*

☐

☐

☐

Saturday/Sunday *(4 & 5)*

☐

☐

☐

> Success is the child of audacity. -Benjamin Disraeli

Top Priority for the Week:

To Do:
- [ ]
- [ ]
- [ ]
- [ ]
- [ ]
- [ ]
- [ ]
- [ ]

Appointments:
- [ ]
- [ ]
- [ ]
- [ ]
- [ ]
- [ ]

Carryover from Prior Week:
- [ ]
- [ ]
- [ ]

Habit Tracker	S	M	T	W	H	F	S

Notes

MAY

s	m	t	w	t	f	s
			1	2	3	4
5	6	7	8	9	10	11
12	13	14	15	16	17	18
19	20	21	22	23	24	25
26	27	28	29	30	31	

May

Sunday	Monday	Tuesday	Wednesday
28	29	30	01
05	06	07	08
12	13	14	15
19	20	21	22
26	27 *Memorial Day*	28	29
02	03	04	05

Thursday	Friday	Saturday	To Do:
02	03	04	☐
			☐
			☐
			☐
09	10	11	☐
			☐
			☐
			☐
16	17	18	☐
			☐
			☐
			☐
23	24	25	☐
			☐
			☐
			☐
30	31	01	☐
			☐
			☐
			☐
06	07	08	☐
			☐
			☐
			☐

May
The Week Of May 6, 2019

Monday *(6)*

☐

☐

☐

Tuesday *(7)*

☐

☐

☐

Wednesday *(8)*

☐

☐

☐

Thursday *(9)*

☐

☐

☐

Friday *(10)*

☐

☐

☐

Saturday/Sunday *(11 & 12)*

☐

☐

☐

If you can't stop thinking about it, don't stop working for it.

Top Priority for the Week:

To Do:
☐   ☐
☐   ☐
☐   ☐
☐   ☐

Appointments:
☐   ☐
☐   ☐
☐   ☐

Carryover from Prior Week:
☐
☐
☐

Habit Tracker	S	M	T	W	H	F	S

Notes

| MAY |

s	m	t	w	t	f	s
			1	2	3	4
5	6	7	8	9	10	11
12	13	14	15	16	17	18
19	20	21	22	23	24	25
26	27	28	29	30	31	

May
The Week Of May 13, 2019

Monday *(13)*

☐

☐

☐

Tuesday *(14)*

☐

☐

☐

Wednesday *(15)*

☐

☐

☐

Thursday *(16)*

☐

☐

☐

Friday *(17)*

☐

☐

☐

Saturday/Sunday *(18 & 19)*

☐

☐

☐

We all have limits. Almost no one reaches theirs.

Top Priority for the Week:

To Do:
☐   ☐
☐   ☐
☐   ☐
☐   ☐

Appointments:
☐   ☐
☐   ☐
☐   ☐

Carryover from Prior Week:
☐
☐
☐

Habit Tracker	S	M	T	W	H	F	S

Notes

MAY
s m t w t f s
1 2 3 4
5 6 7 8 9 10 11
12 13 14 15 16 17 18
19 20 21 22 23 24 25
26 27 28 29 30 31

May
The Week Of May 20, 2019

Monday *(20)*

☐

☐

☐

Tuesday *(21)*

☐

☐

☐

Wednesday *(22)*

☐

☐

☐

Thursday *(23)*

☐

☐

☐

Friday *(24)*

☐

☐

☐

Saturday/Sunday *(25 & 26)*

☐

☐

☐

Excellence is not a skill. It is an attitude. -Ralph Marston

Top Priority for the Week:

To Do:
- [ ]   [ ]
- [ ]   [ ]
- [ ]   [ ]
- [ ]   [ ]

Appointments:
- [ ]   [ ]
- [ ]   [ ]
- [ ]   [ ]

Carryover from Prior Week:
- [ ]
- [ ]
- [ ]

Habit Tracker	S	M	T	W	H	F	S

Notes

MAY

s	m	t	w	t	f	s
			1	2	3	4
5	6	7	8	9	10	11
12	13	14	15	16	17	18
19	20	21	22	23	24	25
26	27	28	29	30	31	

May
The Week Of May 27, 2019

Monday *(27)*

☐

☐

☐

Tuesday *(28)*

☐

☐

☐

Wednesday *(29)*

☐

☐

☐

Thursday *(30)*

☐

☐

☐

Friday *(31)*

☐

☐

☐

Saturday/Sunday *(1 & 2)*

☐

☐

☐

Dream big and dare to fail. -Norman Vaughan

Top Priority for the Week:

To Do:

☐   ☐

☐   ☐

☐   ☐

☐   ☐

Appointments:

☐   ☐

☐   ☐

☐   ☐

Carryover from Prior Week:

☐

☐

☐

Habit Tracker	S	M	T	W	H	F	S

Notes

▌JUNE

s	m	t	w	t	f	s
						1
2	3	4	5	6	7	8
9	10	11	12	13	14	15
16	17	18	19	20	21	22
23	24	25	26	27	28	29
30						

June

Sunday	Monday	Tuesday	Wednesday
26	27	28	29
02	03	04	05
09	10	11	12
16	17	18	19
23	24	25	26
30	01	02	03

Thursday	Friday	Saturday	To Do:
30	31	01	☐
			☐
			☐
06	07	08	☐
			☐
			☐
			☐
13	14	15	☐
			☐
			☐
20	21	22	☐
			☐
			☐
			☐
27	28	29	☐
			☐
			☐
			☐
04	05	06	☐
			☐
			☐

June
The Week Of June 3, 2019

Monday *(3)*

☐

☐

☐

Tuesday *(4)*

☐

☐

☐

Wednesday *(5)*

☐

☐

☐

Thursday *(6)*

☐

☐

☐

Friday *(7)*

☐

☐

☐

Saturday/Sunday *(8 & 9)*

☐

☐

☐

Its kind of fun to do the impossible. -Walt Disney

Top Priority for the Week:

To Do:
☐   ☐

☐   ☐

☐   ☐

☐   ☐

Appointments:
☐   ☐

☐   ☐

☐   ☐

Carryover from Prior Week:
☐

☐

☐

Habit Tracker	S	M	T	W	H	F	S

Notes

▌JUNE

s	m	t	w	t	f	s
						1
2	3	4	5	6	7	8
9	10	11	12	13	14	15
16	17	18	19	20	21	22
23	24	25	26	27	28	29
30						

June
The Week Of June 10, 2019

Monday *(10)*

☐

☐

☐

Tuesday *(11)*

☐

☐

☐

Wednesday *(12)*

☐

☐

☐

Thursday *(13)*

☐

☐

☐

Friday *(14)*

☐

☐

☐

Saturday/Sunday *(15 & 16)*

☐

☐

☐

If you haven't found it yet, keep looking.

Top Priority for the Week:

To Do:
☐   ☐

☐   ☐

☐   ☐

☐   ☐

Appointments:

☐   ☐

☐   ☐

☐   ☐

Carryover from Prior Week:

☐

☐

☐

Habit Tracker	S	M	T	W	H	F	S

Notes

_____

_____

_____

_____

_____

▍ JUNE

s	m	t	w	t	f	s
						1
2	3	4	5	6	7	8
9	10	11	12	13	14	15
16	17	18	19	20	21	22
23	24	25	26	27	28	29
30						

June
The Week Of June 17, 2019

Monday *(17)*

☐

☐

☐

Tuesday *(18)*

☐

☐

☐

Wednesday *(19)*

☐

☐

☐

Thursday *(20)*

☐

☐

☐

Friday *(21)*

☐

☐

☐

Saturday/Sunday *(22 & 23)*

☐

☐

☐

Success is most often achieved by those who don't know
that failure is inevitable. -Coco Chanel

Top Priority for the Week:

To Do:
☐   ☐
☐   ☐
☐   ☐
☐   ☐

Appointments:
☐   ☐
☐   ☐
☐   ☐

Carryover from Prior Week:
☐
☐
☐

Habit Tracker	S	M	T	W	H	F	S

Notes

▌JUNE

s	m	t	w	t	f	s
						1
2	3	4	5	6	7	8
9	10	11	12	13	14	15
16	17	18	19	20	21	22
23	24	25	26	27	28	29
30						

June
The Week Of June 24, 2019

Monday *(24)*

☐

☐

☐

Tuesday *(25)*

☐

☐

☐

Wednesday *(26)*

☐

☐

☐

Thursday *(27)*

☐

☐

☐

Friday *(28)*

☐

☐

☐

Saturday/Sunday *(29 & 30)*

☐

☐

☐

Once you start to see results, it becomes an addiction.

Top Priority for the Week:

To Do:
- ☐
- ☐
- ☐
- ☐

- ☐
- ☐
- ☐
- ☐

Appointments:
- ☐
- ☐
- ☐

- ☐
- ☐
- ☐

Carryover from Prior Week:
- ☐
- ☐
- ☐

Habit Tracker	S	M	T	W	H	F	S

Notes

JULY

s	m	t	w	t	f	s
	1	2	3	4	5	6
7	8	9	10	11	12	13
14	15	16	17	18	19	20
21	22	23	24	25	26	27
28	29	30	31			

July

Sunday	Monday	Tuesday	Wednesday
30	01	02	03
07	08	09	10
14	15	16	17
21	22	23	24
28	29	30	31
04	05	06	07

Thursday	Friday	Saturday	To Do:
04 *Independence Day*	05	06	☐
			☐
			☐
11	12	13	☐
			☐
			☐
			☐
18	19	20	☐
			☐
			☐
			☐
25	26	27	☐
			☐
			☐
			☐
01	02	03	☐
			☐
			☐
			☐
08	09	10	☐
			☐
			☐
			☐

July
The Week Of July 1, 2019

Monday *(1)*

☐

☐

☐

Tuesday *(2)*

☐

☐

☐

Wednesday *(3)*

☐

☐

☐

Thursday *(4)*

☐

☐

☐

Friday *(5)*

☐

☐

☐

Saturday/Sunday *(6 & 7)*

☐

☐

☐

> Nothing is either good or bad but thinking makes it so.
> -Shakespeare

Top Priority for the Week:

___

To Do:

☐   ☐

☐   ☐

☐   ☐

☐   ☐

Appointments:

☐   ☐

☐   ☐

☐   ☐

Carryover from Prior Week:

☐

☐

☐

Habit Tracker	S	M	T	W	H	F	S

Notes

___

___

___

___

___

▌JULY

s	m	t	w	t	f	s
	1	2	3	4	5	6
7	8	9	10	11	12	13
14	15	16	17	18	19	20
21	22	23	24	25	26	27
28	29	30	31			

July
The Week Of July 8, 2019

Monday *(8)*

☐

☐

☐

Tuesday *(9)*

☐

☐

☐

Wednesday *(10)*

☐

☐

☐

Thursday *(11)*

☐

☐

☐

Friday *(12)*

☐

☐

☐

Saturday/Sunday *(13 & 14)*

☐

☐

☐

Wherever you go, go with all your heart. -Confucius

Top Priority for the Week:

To Do:

- [ ]
- [ ]
- [ ]
- [ ]
- [ ]
- [ ]
- [ ]
- [ ]

Appointments:

- [ ]
- [ ]
- [ ]
- [ ]
- [ ]
- [ ]

Carryover from Prior Week:

- [ ]
- [ ]
- [ ]

Habit Tracker	S	M	T	W	H	F	S

Notes

| JULY |
s	m	t	w	t	f	s
	1	2	3	4	5	6
7	8	9	10	11	12	13
14	15	16	17	18	19	20
21	22	23	24	25	26	27
28	29	30	31			

July
The Week Of July 15, 2019

Monday *(15)*

- [ ]
- [ ]
- [ ]

Tuesday *(16)*

- [ ]
- [ ]
- [ ]

Wednesday *(17)*

- [ ]
- [ ]
- [ ]

Thursday *(:Day20.:)*

- [ ]
- [ ]
- [ ]

Friday *(19)*

- [ ]
- [ ]
- [ ]

Saturday/Sunday *(20 & 21)*

- [ ]
- [ ]
- [ ]

Fortune and love favor the brave. -Ovid

Top Priority for the Week:

To Do:

☐　　　　　　　　　☐

☐　　　　　　　　　☐

☐　　　　　　　　　☐

☐　　　　　　　　　☐

Appointments:

☐　　　　　　　　　☐

☐　　　　　　　　　☐

☐　　　　　　　　　☐

Carryover from Prior Week:

☐

☐

☐

Habit Tracker	S	M	T	W	H	F	S

Notes

_____

_____

_____

_____

_____

▌JULY

s	m	t	w	t	f	s
		1	2	3	4	5	6
7	8	9	10	11	12	13
14	15	16	17	18	19	20
21	22	23	24	25	26	27
28	29	30	31			

July
The Week Of July 22, 2019

Monday *(22)*

☐

☐

☐

Tuesday *(23)*

☐

☐

☐

Wednesday *(24)*

☐

☐

☐

Thursday *(25)*

☐

☐

☐

Friday *(26)*

☐

☐

☐

Saturday/Sunday *(27 & 28)*

☐

☐

☐

Whether you think you can, or you think you can't
-- you're right. -Henry Ford

Top Priority for the Week:

To Do:
☐   ☐

☐   ☐

☐   ☐

☐   ☐

Appointments:

☐   ☐

☐   ☐

☐   ☐

Carryover from Prior Week:

☐

☐

☐

Habit Tracker	S	M	T	W	H	F	S

Notes

▌JULY

s	m	t	w	t	f	s
	1	2	3	4	5	6
7	8	9	10	11	12	13
14	15	16	17	18	19	20
21	22	23	24	25	26	27
28	29	30	31			

July
The Week Of July 29, 2019

Monday *(29)*

☐

☐

☐

Tuesday *(30)*

☐

☐

☐

Wednesday *(31)*

☐

☐

☐

Thursday *(1)*

☐

☐

☐

Friday *(2)*

☐

☐

☐

Saturday/Sunday *(3 & 4)*

☐

☐

☐

Diligence is the mother of good fortune. -Cervantes

Top Priority for the Week:

To Do:
☐   ☐

☐   ☐

☐   ☐

☐   ☐

Appointments:

☐   ☐

☐   ☐

☐   ☐

Carryover from Prior Week:

☐

☐

☐

Habit Tracker	*S*	*M*	*T*	*W*	*H*	*F*	*S*

Notes

▌AUGUST

s	m	t	w	t	f	s
				1	2	3
4	5	6	7	8	9	10
11	12	13	14	15	16	17
18	19	20	21	22	23	24
25	26	27	28	29	30	31

August

Sunday	Monday	Tuesday	Wednesday
28	29	30	31
04	05	06	07
11	12	13	14
18	19	20	21
25	26	27	28
01	02 *Labor Day*	03	04

Thursday	Friday	Saturday	To Do:
01	02	03	☐
			☐
			☐
08	09	10	☐
			☐
			☐
			☐
15	16	17	☐
			☐
			☐
			☐
22	23	24	☐
			☐
			☐
			☐
29	30	31	☐
			☐
			☐
			☐
05	06	07	☐
			☐
			☐
			☐

August
The Week Of August 5, 2019

Monday *(5)*

☐

☐

☐

Tuesday *(6)*

☐

☐

☐

Wednesday *(7)*

☐

☐

☐

Thursday *(8)*

☐

☐

☐

Friday *(9)*

☐

☐

☐

Saturday/Sunday *(10 & 11)*

☐

☐

☐

Top Priority for the Week:

To Do:
- [ ]
- [ ]
- [ ]
- [ ]

- [ ]
- [ ]
- [ ]
- [ ]

Appointments:
- [ ]
- [ ]
- [ ]

- [ ]
- [ ]
- [ ]

Carryover from Prior Week:
- [ ]
- [ ]
- [ ]

Habit Tracker	S	M	T	W	H	F	S

Notes

AUGUST

s	m	t	w	t	f	s
				1	2	3
4	5	6	7	8	9	10
11	12	13	14	15	16	17
18	19	20	21	22	23	24
25	26	27	28	29	30	31

August
The Week Of August 12, 2019

Monday *(12)*

☐

☐

☐

Tuesday *(13)*

☐

☐

☐

Wednesday *(14)*

☐

☐

☐

Thursday *(15)*

☐

☐

☐

Friday *(16)*

☐

☐

☐

Saturday/Sunday *(17 & 18)*

☐

☐

☐

To save all we must risk all. -Friedrich Von Schiller

Top Priority for the Week:

To Do:
☐   ☐

☐   ☐

☐   ☐

☐   ☐

Appointments:

☐   ☐

☐   ☐

☐   ☐

Carryover from Prior Week:

☐

☐

☐

Habit Tracker	S	M	T	W	H	F	S

Notes

▌AUGUST

s	m	t	w	t	f	s
				1	2	3
4	5	6	7	8	9	10
11	12	13	14	15	16	17
18	19	20	21	22	23	24
25	26	27	28	29	30	31

August
The Week Of August 19, 2019

Monday *(19)*

- [ ]
- [ ]
- [ ]

Tuesday *(20)*

- [ ]
- [ ]
- [ ]

Wednesday *(21)*

- [ ]
- [ ]
- [ ]

Thursday *(22)*

- [ ]
- [ ]
- [ ]

Friday *(23)*

- [ ]
- [ ]
- [ ]

Saturday/Sunday *(24 & 25)*

- [ ]
- [ ]
- [ ]

A No. 2 pencil and a dream can take you anywhere.
-Joyce Meyer

Top Priority for the Week:

To Do:
- [ ]   [ ]
- [ ]   [ ]
- [ ]   [ ]
- [ ]   [ ]

Appointments:
- [ ]   [ ]
- [ ]   [ ]
- [ ]   [ ]

Carryover from Prior Week:
- [ ]
- [ ]
- [ ]

Habit Tracker	S	M	T	W	H	F	S

Notes

AUGUST						
s	m	t	w	t	f	s
				1	2	3
4	5	6	7	8	9	10
11	12	13	14	15	16	17
18	19	20	21	22	23	24
25	26	27	28	29	30	31

August
The Week Of August 26, 2019

Monday *(26)*

☐

☐

☐

Tuesday *(27)*

☐

☐

☐

Wednesday *(28)*

☐

☐

☐

Thursday *(29)*

☐

☐

☐

Friday *(30)*

☐

☐

☐

Saturday/Sunday *(31 & 1)*

☐

☐

☐

A minute now is better than a minute later.

Top Priority for the Week:

To Do:

☐   ☐

☐   ☐

☐   ☐

☐   ☐

Appointments:

☐   ☐

☐   ☐

☐   ☐

Carryover from Prior Week:

☐

☐

☐

Habit Tracker	S	M	T	W	H	F	S

Notes

SEPTEMBER						
s	m	t	w	t	f	s
1	2	3	4	5	6	7
8	9	10	11	12	13	14
15	16	17	18	19	20	21
22	23	24	25	26	27	28
29	30					

September

Sunday	Monday	Tuesday	Wednesday
01	02 *Labor Day*	03	04
08	09	10	11
15	16	17	18
22	23	24	25
29	30	01	02
06	07	08	09

Thursday	Friday	Saturday	To Do:
05	06	07	☐
			☐
			☐
12	13	14	☐
			☐
			☐
			☐
19	20	21	☐
			☐
			☐
			☐
26	27	28	☐
			☐
			☐
			☐
03	04	05	☐
			☐
			☐
			☐
10	11	12	☐
			☐
			☐
			☐

September
The Week Of September 2, 2019

Monday *(2)*

☐

☐

☐

Tuesday *(3)*

☐

☐

☐

Wednesday *(4)*

☐

☐

☐

Thursday *(5)*

☐

☐

☐

Friday *(6)*

☐

☐

☐

Saturday/Sunday *(7 & 8)*

☐

☐

☐

Learn from yesterday, live for today, hope for tomorrow.

Top Priority for the Week:

To Do:
☐   ☐

☐   ☐

☐   ☐

☐   ☐

Appointments:
☐   ☐

☐   ☐

☐   ☐

Carryover from Prior Week:
☐

☐

☐

Habit Tracker	S	M	T	W	H	F	S

Notes

SEPTEMBER
s	m	t	w	t	f	s
1	2	3	4	5	6	7
8	9	10	11	12	13	14
15	16	17	18	19	20	21
22	23	24	25	26	27	28
29	30					

September

The Week Of September 9, 2019

Monday *(9)*

☐

☐

☐

Tuesday *(10)*

☐

☐

☐

Wednesday *(11)*

☐

☐

☐

Thursday *(12)*

☐

☐

☐

Friday *(13)*

☐

☐

☐

Saturday/Sunday *(14 & 15)*

☐

☐

☐

Well done is better than well said. -Benjamin Franklin

Top Priority for the Week:

To Do:
- [ ]   [ ]
- [ ]   [ ]
- [ ]   [ ]
- [ ]   [ ]

Appointments:
- [ ]   [ ]
- [ ]   [ ]
- [ ]   [ ]

Carryover from Prior Week:
- [ ]
- [ ]
- [ ]

Habit Tracker	S	M	T	W	H	F	S

Notes

SEPTEMBER

s	m	t	w	t	f	s
1	2	3	4	5	6	7
8	9	10	11	12	13	14
15	16	17	18	19	20	21
22	23	24	25	26	27	28
29	30					

September
The Week Of September 16, 2019

Monday (16)

☐

☐

☐

Tuesday (17)

☐

☐

☐

Wednesday (18)

☐

☐

☐

Thursday (19)

☐

☐

☐

Friday (20)

☐

☐

☐

Saturday/Sunday (21 & 22)

☐

☐

☐

When I let go of what I am, I become what I might be.
-Lao Tzu

Top Priority for the Week:

To Do:
- [ ]   [ ]
- [ ]   [ ]
- [ ]   [ ]
- [ ]   [ ]

Appointments:
- [ ]   [ ]
- [ ]   [ ]
- [ ]   [ ]

Carryover from Prior Week:
- [ ]
- [ ]
- [ ]

Habit Tracker	S	M	T	W	H	F	S

Notes

SEPTEMBER

s	m	t	w	t	f	s
1	2	3	4	5	6	7
8	9	10	11	12	13	14
15	16	17	18	19	20	21
22	23	24	25	26	27	28
29	30					

September
The Week Of September 23, 2019

Monday *(23)*

- [ ]
- [ ]
- [ ]

Tuesday *(24)*

- [ ]
- [ ]
- [ ]

Wednesday *(25)*

- [ ]
- [ ]
- [ ]

Thursday *(26)*

- [ ]
- [ ]
- [ ]

Friday *(27)*

- [ ]
- [ ]
- [ ]

Saturday/Sunday *(28 & 29)*

- [ ]
- [ ]
- [ ]

> The future belongs to those who believe in the beauty of their dreams. -Eleanor Roosevelt

Top Priority for the Week:

To Do:
- ☐
- ☐
- ☐
- ☐

- ☐
- ☐
- ☐
- ☐

Appointments:
- ☐
- ☐
- ☐

- ☐
- ☐
- ☐

Carryover from Prior Week:
- ☐
- ☐
- ☐

Habit Tracker	S	M	T	W	H	F	S

Notes

SEPTEMBER

s	m	t	w	t	f	s
1	2	3	4	5	6	7
8	9	10	11	12	13	14
15	16	17	18	19	20	21
22	23	24	25	26	27	28
29	30					

September
The Week Of September 30, 2019

Monday *(30)*

☐

☐

☐

Tuesday *(1)*

☐

☐

☐

Wednesday *(2)*

☐

☐

☐

Thursday *(3)*

☐

☐

☐

Friday *(4)*

☐

☐

☐

Saturday/Sunday *(5 & 6)*

☐

☐

☐

The secret of having it all is believing you already do.

Top Priority for the Week:

To Do:
- ☐
- ☐
- ☐
- ☐

- ☐
- ☐
- ☐
- ☐

Appointments:

- ☐
- ☐
- ☐

- ☐
- ☐
- ☐

Carryover from Prior Week:

- ☐
- ☐
- ☐

Habit Tracker	S	M	T	W	H	F	S

Notes

OCTOBER						
s	m	t	w	t	f	s
		1	2	3	4	5
6	7	8	9	10	11	12
13	14	15	16	17	18	19
20	21	22	23	24	25	26
27	28	29	30	31		

October

Sunday	Monday	Tuesday	Wednesday
29	30	01	02
06	07	08	09
13	14 *Columbus Day*	15	16
20	21	22	23
27	28	29	30
03	04	05	06

Thursday	Friday	Saturday	To Do:
03	04	05	☐
			☐
			☐
10	11	12	☐
			☐
			☐
			☐
17	18	19	☐
			☐
			☐
			☐
24	25	26	☐
			☐
			☐
			☐
31 Halloween	01	02	☐
			☐
			☐
			☐
07	08	09	☐
			☐
			☐
			☐

October

The Week Of October 7, 2019

Monday *(7)*

☐

☐

☐

Tuesday *(8)*

☐

☐

☐

Wednesday *(9)*

☐

☐

☐

Thursday *(10)*

☐

☐

☐

Friday *(11)*

☐

☐

☐

Saturday/Sunday *(12 & 13)*

☐

☐

☐

Don't regret the past, just learn from it. -Ben Ipock

Top Priority for the Week:

To Do:
☐   ☐
☐   ☐
☐   ☐
☐   ☐

Appointments:
☐   ☐
☐   ☐
☐   ☐

Carryover from Prior Week:
☐
☐
☐

Habit Tracker	S	M	T	W	H	F	S

Notes

OCTOBER

s	m	t	w	t	f	s
		1	2	3	4	5
6	7	8	9	10	11	12
13	14	15	16	17	18	19
20	21	22	23	24	25	26
27	28	29	30	31		

October
The Week Of October 14, 2019

Monday *(14)*

- [ ]
- [ ]
- [ ]

Tuesday *(:Day2289:)*

- [ ]
- [ ]
- [ ]

Wednesday *(16)*

- [ ]
- [ ]
- [ ]

Thursday *(17)*

- [ ]
- [ ]
- [ ]

Friday *(18)*

- [ ]
- [ ]
- [ ]

Saturday/Sunday *(19 & 20)*

- [ ]
- [ ]
- [ ]

It does not matter how slowly you go as long as you
do not stop. -Confucius

Top Priority for the Week:

To Do:
☐ ☐
☐ ☐
☐ ☐
☐ ☐

Appointments:
☐ ☐
☐ ☐
☐ ☐

Carryover from Prior Week:
☐
☐
☐

Habit Tracker	S	M	T	W	H	F	S

Notes

OCTOBER

s	m	t	w	t	f	s
		1	2	3	4	5
6	7	8	9	10	11	12
13	14	15	16	17	18	19
20	21	22	23	24	25	26
27	28	29	30	31		

October
The Week Of October 21, 2019

Monday *(21)*

☐

☐

☐

Tuesday *(22)*

☐

☐

☐

Wednesday *(23)*

☐

☐

☐

Thursday *(24)*

☐

☐

☐

Friday *(25)*

☐

☐

☐

Saturday/Sunday *(26 & 27)*

☐

☐

☐

In order to succeed, we must first believe that we can.
-Nikos Kazantzakis

Top Priority for the Week:

To Do:

☐   ☐

☐   ☐

☐   ☐

☐   ☐

Appointments:

☐   ☐

☐   ☐

☐   ☐

Carryover from Prior Week:

☐

☐

☐

Habit Tracker	S	M	T	W	H	F	S

Notes

▌OCTOBER

s	m	t	w	t	f	s
		1	2	3	4	5
6	7	8	9	10	11	12
13	14	15	16	17	18	19
20	21	22	23	24	25	26
27	28	29	30	31		

October
The Week Of October 28, 2019

Monday *(28)*

☐

☐

☐

Tuesday *(29)*

☐

☐

☐

Wednesday *(30)*

☐

☐

☐

Thursday *(31)*

☐

☐

☐

Friday *(1)*

☐

☐

☐

Saturday/Sunday *(2 & 3)*

☐

☐

☐

> If you want to succeed you should strike out on new paths,
> rather than travel the worn paths of accepted success.
> -J.D. Rockefeller

Top Priority for the Week:

To Do:
- [ ]   [ ]
- [ ]   [ ]
- [ ]   [ ]
- [ ]   [ ]

Appointments:
- [ ]   [ ]
- [ ]   [ ]
- [ ]   [ ]

Carryover from Prior Week:
- [ ]
- [ ]
- [ ]

Habit Tracker	S	M	T	W	H	F	S

Notes

NOVEMBER						
s	m	t	w	t	f	s
					1	2
3	4	5	6	7	8	9
10	11	12	13	14	15	16
17	18	19	20	21	22	23
24	25	26	27	28	29	30

November

Sunday	Monday	Tuesday	Wednesday
27	28	29	30
03	04	05	06
10	11 *Veterans Day*	12	13
17	18	19	20
24	25	26	27
01	02	03	04

Thursday	Friday	Saturday	To Do:
31 _Halloween_	01	02	☐ ☐ ☐
07	08	09	☐ ☐ ☐ ☐
14	15	16	☐ ☐ ☐ ☐
21	22	23	☐ ☐ ☐
28 _Thanksgiving Day_	29	30	☐ ☐ ☐ ☐
05	06	07	☐ ☐ ☐

November

The Week Of November 4, 2019

Monday *(4)*

☐

☐

☐

Tuesday *(5)*

☐

☐

☐

Wednesday *(6)*

☐

☐

☐

Thursday *(7)*

☐

☐

☐

Friday *(8)*

☐

☐

☐

Saturday/Sunday *(9 & 10)*

☐

☐

☐

Genius is 1% inspiration, 99% perspiration. -Thomas Edison

Top Priority for the Week:

To Do:
- ☐   ☐
- ☐   ☐
- ☐   ☐
- ☐   ☐

Appointments:
- ☐   ☐
- ☐   ☐
- ☐   ☐

Carryover from Prior Week:
- ☐
- ☐
- ☐

Habit Tracker	S	M	T	W	H	F	S

Notes

NOVEMBER						
s	m	t	w	t	f	s
					1	2
3	4	5	6	7	8	9
10	11	12	13	14	15	16
17	18	19	20	21	22	23
24	25	26	27	28	29	30

November
The Week Of November 11, 2019

Monday *(11)*

☐

☐

☐

Tuesday *(12)*

☐

☐

☐

Wednesday *(13)*

☐

☐

☐

Thursday *(14)*

☐

☐

☐

Friday *(15)*

☐

☐

☐

Saturday/Sunday *(16 & 17)*

☐

☐

☐

> Don't be afraid to give up the good and go for the great.
> -J.D. Rockefeller

Top Priority for the Week:

To Do:
- [ ]
- [ ]
- [ ]
- [ ]
- [ ]
- [ ]
- [ ]
- [ ]

Appointments:
- [ ]
- [ ]
- [ ]
- [ ]
- [ ]
- [ ]

Carryover from Prior Week:
- [ ]
- [ ]
- [ ]

Habit Tracker	S	M	T	W	H	F	S

Notes

_____

_____

_____

_____

_____

NOVEMBER

s	m	t	w	t	f	s
					1	2
3	4	5	6	7	8	9
10	11	12	13	14	15	16
17	18	19	20	21	22	23
24	25	26	27	28	29	30

November
The Week Of November 18, 2019

Monday *(18)*

- [ ]
- [ ]
- [ ]

Tuesday *(19)*

- [ ]
- [ ]
- [ ]

Wednesday *(20)*

- [ ]
- [ ]
- [ ]

Thursday *(21)*

- [ ]
- [ ]
- [ ]

Friday *(22)*

- [ ]
- [ ]
- [ ]

Saturday/Sunday *(23 & 24)*

- [ ]
- [ ]
- [ ]

> Your personal philosophy is the greatest determining factor
> in how your life works out. -Jim Rohn

Top Priority for the Week:

To Do:

☐   ☐

☐   ☐

☐   ☐

☐   ☐

Appointments:

☐   ☐

☐   ☐

☐   ☐

Carryover from Prior Week:

☐

☐

☐

Habit Tracker	S	M	T	W	H	F	S

Notes

NOVEMBER

s	m	t	w	t	f	s
					1	2
3	4	5	6	7	8	9
10	11	12	13	14	15	16
17	18	19	20	21	22	23
24	25	26	27	28	29	30

November

The Week Of November 25, 2019

Monday *(25)*

☐

☐

☐

Tuesday *(26)*

☐

☐

☐

Wednesday *(27)*

☐

☐

☐

Thursday *(28)*

☐

☐

☐

Friday *(29)*

☐

☐

☐

Saturday/Sunday *(30 & 1)*

☐

☐

☐

If you have never failed you have never lived.

Top Priority for the Week:

To Do:
- ☐   ☐
- ☐   ☐
- ☐   ☐
- ☐   ☐

Appointments:
- ☐   ☐
- ☐   ☐
- ☐   ☐

Carryover from Prior Week:
- ☐
- ☐
- ☐

Habit Tracker	S	M	T	W	H	F	S

Notes

DECEMBER						
s	m	t	w	t	f	s
1	2	3	4	5	6	7
8	9	10	11	12	13	14
15	16	17	18	19	20	21
22	23	24	25	26	27	28
29	30	31				

December

Sunday	Monday	Tuesday	Wednesday
01	02	03	04
08	09	10	11
15	16	17	18
22	23	24	25 Christmas Day
29	30	31	01 New Year's Day
05	06	07	08

Thursday	Friday	Saturday	To Do:
05	06	07	☐
			☐
			☐
			☐
12	13	14	☐
			☐
			☐
19	20	21	☐
			☐
			☐
			☐
26	27	28	☐
			☐
			☐
			☐
02	03	04	☐
			☐
			☐
			☐
09	10	11	☐
			☐
			☐
			☐

December

The Week Of December 2, 2019

Monday *(2)*

- [ ]
- [ ]
- [ ]

Tuesday *(3)*

- [ ]
- [ ]
- [ ]

Wednesday *(4)*

- [ ]
- [ ]
- [ ]

Thursday *(5)*

- [ ]
- [ ]
- [ ]

Friday *(6)*

- [ ]
- [ ]
- [ ]

Saturday/Sunday *(7 & 8)*

- [ ]
- [ ]
- [ ]

Beginnings are always messy. -John Galsworth

Top Priority for the Week:

To Do:

☐   ☐

☐   ☐

☐   ☐

☐   ☐

Appointments:

☐   ☐

☐   ☐

☐   ☐

Carryover from Prior Week:

☐

☐

☐

Habit Tracker	S	M	T	W	H	F	S

Notes

DECEMBER

s	m	t	w	t	f	s
1	2	3	4	5	6	7
8	9	10	11	12	13	14
15	16	17	18	19	20	21
22	23	24	25	26	27	28
29	30	31				

December
The Week Of December 9, 2019

Monday *(9)*

☐

☐

☐

Tuesday *(10)*

☐

☐

☐

Wednesday *(11)*

☐

☐

☐

Thursday *(12)*

☐

☐

☐

Friday *(13)*

☐

☐

☐

Saturday/Sunday *(14 & 15)*

☐

☐

☐

Believe you can and you're halfway there.
-Theodore Roosevelt

Top Priority for the Week:

To Do:

☐   ☐

☐   ☐

☐   ☐

☐   ☐

Appointments:

☐   ☐

☐   ☐

☐   ☐

Carryover from Prior Week:

☐

☐

☐

Habit Tracker	S	M	T	W	H	F	S

Notes

DECEMBER

s	m	t	w	t	f	s
1	2	3	4	5	6	7
8	9	10	11	12	13	14
15	16	17	18	19	20	21
22	23	24	25	26	27	28
29	30	31				

December
The Week Of December 16, 2019

Monday *(16)*

☐

☐

☐

Tuesday *(17)*

☐

☐

☐

Wednesday *(18)*

☐

☐

☐

Thursday *(19)*

☐

☐

☐

Friday *(20)*

☐

☐

☐

Saturday/Sunday *(21 & 22)*

☐

☐

☐

The only limit to our realization of tomorrow will be our doubts of today. -Franklin D. Roosevelt

Top Priority for the Week:

To Do:
☐   ☐

☐   ☐

☐   ☐

☐   ☐

Appointments:
☐   ☐

☐   ☐

☐   ☐

Carryover from Prior Week:
☐

☐

☐

Habit Tracker	S	M	T	W	H	F	S

Notes

DECEMBER

s	m	t	w	t	f	s
1	2	3	4	5	6	7
8	9	10	11	12	13	14
15	16	17	18	19	20	21
22	23	24	25	26	27	28
29	30	31				

December
The Week Of December 23, 2019

Monday *(23)*

- ☐
- ☐
- ☐

Tuesday *(24)*

- ☐
- ☐
- ☐

Wednesday *(25)*

- ☐
- ☐
- ☐

Thursday *(26)*

- ☐
- ☐
- ☐

Friday *(27)*

- ☐
- ☐
- ☐

Saturday/Sunday *(28 & 29)*

- ☐
- ☐
- ☐

Dream as if you'll live forever. Live as if you'll die today.
-James Dean

Top Priority for the Week:

To Do:
☐   ☐
☐   ☐
☐   ☐
☐   ☐

Appointments:
☐   ☐
☐   ☐
☐   ☐

Carryover from Prior Week:
☐
☐
☐

Habit Tracker	S	M	T	W	H	F	S

Notes

DECEMBER

s	m	t	w	t	f	s
1	2	3	4	5	6	7
8	9	10	11	12	13	14
15	16	17	18	19	20	21
22	23	24	25	26	27	28
29	30	31				

December
The Week Of December 30, 2019

Monday *(30)*

☐

☐

☐

Tuesday *(31)*

☐

☐

☐

Wednesday *(1)*

☐

☐

☐

Thursday *(2)*

☐

☐

☐

Friday *(3)*

☐

☐

☐

Saturday/Sunday *(4 & 5)*

☐

☐

☐

You are young at any age if you're planning for tomorrow.

Top Priority for the Week:

To Do:
☐   ☐
☐   ☐
☐   ☐
☐   ☐

Appointments:
☐   ☐
☐   ☐
☐   ☐

Carryover from Prior Week:
☐
☐
☐

Habit Tracker	S	M	T	W	H	F	S

Notes

JANUARY

s	m	t	w	t	f	s
			1	2	3	4
5	6	7	8	9	10	11
12	13	14	15	16	17	18
19	20	21	22	23	24	25
26	27	28	29	30	31	

HABIT/GOAL TRACKER

Start Date:

Habit/Goal	1	2	3	4	5	6	7	8	9	10	11	12	13	14	15	16	17	18	19	20	21	22	23	24	25

Support comes in many forms (purchases, likes, and especially Amazon reviews). We truly appreciate all the support our patrons have provided us. As a "Thank You" for your continuing support and as a token of our appreciation, below is an QR Code for you to download a **free** "Get Shit Done" 8x10 printable wall art (PDF)*:

For Personal Use Only